Using storytelling to talk about...

Health & Self care

Stories, Poems and Activities to teach and learn in the Early Years

Contents

Introduction	2
Storytelling tips	3
Being active: Star Jumpers Club	4 STORY
Different foods: At the Market	10 SONG
Keeping safe: Zig Gets Lost	16 STORY
Getting clean: What Shall I Do?	24 SONG
Using a hankie: Snozzle the Sneezing Giant	30 STORY
Caring for our teeth: Our Teeth	36 POEM
Dressing for the weather: Changing Weather	42 STORY
Different clothes fastenings: All Done Up	48 POEM
EYFS Learning Areas Reference Chart	54
Storytelling assessment record	55
Observation suggestions	56
Observation record	57

Published by Practical Pre-School Books, A Division of MA Education Ltd, St Jude's Church, Dulwich Road, Herne Hill, London, SE24 0PB.
Tel: 020 7738 5454 www.practicalpreschoolbooks.com

© MA Education Ltd 2021

Design: Mary Holmes **fonthill**creative 01722 717036

All images © MA Education Ltd. with the exception of p13 © Boggy/Adobe Stock; p27 © MARY/Adobe Stock. Border images; p5-6 © stas111/Adobe Stock; p11 © mariabo/Adobe Stock; p17-18 © lar01joka/Adobe Stock; p25 © Olga Moonlight/Adobe Stock; p37 © olllikebaloon/Adobe Stock; p43 © chica/Adobe Stock; p49 © AlexanderZam/Adobe Stock.

All rights reserved. No part of this publication may be reproduced, stored in a retrieval system, or transmitted by any means, electronic, mechanical, photocopied or otherwise, without the prior permission of the publisher.

ISBN 978-1-912611-37-9

Introduction

About the series

This book is part of the 'Using storytelling to talk about…' series which gives teaching practitioners the support and resources to develop and use storytelling and poetry/song performance skills in the Early Years Foundation Stage. Each book has specifically-written short interactive stories and poems/songs that are linked to the three different learning and development areas, 'Personal, social and emotional development', 'Understanding the world' and 'Health and self care'. The prime area 'Communication and language' is a running thread throughout all five books.

How to use the series

All the stories and poems/songs deal with issues or experiences that would be familiar to young children. They are short, interactive and simple to perform, with repetitive texts that offer the children the opportunity to respond and join in at their own level of understanding and language development.

The stories and poems/songs can be used in a variety of ways, for example:
- as a 'Let's have a short story (poem/song)' session at a set time each day or on a particular day of the week.
- as a way to help introduce, support or consolidate a topic or theme.
- by choosing a themed story/poem to support or discuss a particular issue, e.g. sharing.
- as an assembly or class performance resource.
- as a book corner recording for play sessions or quiet time.

How to use this book

This book contains eight themed sections that are linked to different early learning goals listed in the focused learning and development area. Each section has a story or a poem icon to show what type of text it is. Use the contents page to select the theme or type of text that you require.

Each section is divided into the following parts:

A. Teacher's notes

- **Theme name:** main learning skill or idea focus behind the story or poem/song and accompanying activities.
- **EYFS learning objectives:** relevant early learning goals from the book's main learning and development area.
- **What you need:** list of resources such as props, images/pictures, puppets and resource sheets.

Before the story or poem/song
- **Getting ready:** tips on what resources to collect, prepare and have ready in advance.
- **Introducing the story or poem/song:** suggestions on how to stimulate the children's curiosity and imagination about the theme, story or poem, e.g. telling and sharing an experience, introducing a character puppet and using props or images.
- **Performance suggestions:** suggestions on how to tell or perform a story or poem/song, e.g. body movements, use of voice and child participation ideas.

After the story or poem/song

These two parts are designed as springboards for further exploration and discussion about the story or poem/song as well as its theme. They could be carried out straight after the story or poem/rhyme or over several days or weeks.
- **Ideas to reinforce the theme:** discussion ideas, activities and question examples to help consolidate the children's understanding and response to the story or poem/song and its main theme.
- **Consolidation activities:** interactive activities to reinforce the story or poem/song and its theme, e.g. using puppets, circle games, music, performance ideas, role play, parachute games and display suggestions.

B. The story or poem/song texts

Body and voice actions suggestions are included for some of the stories and poems/songs. As you get to know the stories and poems/songs, you may want to add in your own ideas and actions.

C. Related activities within the learning environment

A mix of child-led and adult–led cross-curricular activities relating to the story or poem/song and its theme. The activities can be carried out within activity stations, play or in specific learning sessions. Areas include: literacy, mathematics, art and craft, environment, small world play.

D. Resource sheets

Most of the stories and poems/songs have character or picture images. These can be copied onto card, laminated and used as puppets or as story support. Other resource sheets include games, activity cards or templates.

Other resources

Storytelling and performance evaluation record
Use this record to self-evaluate your storytelling skills and performance after each of the stories and poems/songs and for future sessions.

Observation suggestions and chart
Use 'Observation suggestions' and 'Observation chart' as an assessment guide to help you identify and note the developing skills, knowledge and attitudes of individuals or groups of children.

Storytelling tips

Preparation

One of the most important elements of story telling and poem/song performance is good preparation. Areas to consider before you see the children are:

1. Choosing a place to read or perform

Choose a comfortable and spacious area to tell stories or perform poems and songs. This could be in a book corner or a place where there is a big rug for the children to sit on. Make sure that there is room for the children to move if they will need to use body actions.

2. Look, read and learn the texts

a. Reading the text - If you prefer to read the text to the children, practise reading it out loud several times on your own. Note any need for voice intonation and expression and simple body actions as well as repetitive words or phrases that the children could join in with you.

b. Learning a story or poem/song
- Read the story or poem/song out loud to yourself several times so you get to know the plot, characters, actions, voices and repetitive texts.
- Split the story or verses into easy sections to learn off by heart.
- You don't have to learn it exactly word for word but try and learn the repetitive text and choruses.
- Story memory aid: Have the skeleton of the story with the main repetitive words/phrases by your side or put it into a 'prompt envelope'. If you forget the story, tell the children that a character has sent you a letter or card about what happened next.
- Poem/song memory aid: Have the verses on a sheet of paper near you or add the verses onto the storyboard so you can read them if needed.

c. Props
Use props to introduce a story or poem/song, enhance the telling and message, encourage interactive participation by the children or aid discussion after the telling.

Prepare or collect your props before the session and plan out how they will be used. Have them close at hand and if possible away from the children's reach. If you need to show a number of props then make sure they are laid out in the right order so that you don't need to work out where each one is while you are performing.

When selecting props, think about the story or poem/song and decide which props would work well, e.g. a bucket and spade for a sandcastle story.

d. A special story and rhyme basket/box
Have a story basket (e.g. picnic hamper) or a box with a lid in which to store the props suggested in the story or poem/song. Over time, the children will become eager to find out what is in the basket/box for that session. Keep them guessing or offer little clues, e.g. In the basket is something we can use to build sandcastles. What is it?

e. Story board - a visual aid
Some young children find visual images help reinforce story events or characters. These are especially useful for children who speak English as a second language. One way to do this, is to have a good sized storyboard in which you can attach pictures and characters (see Resource Sheets) before and during the performance or telling. Attach a sticky backing so they can stick easily onto the board.

2. Starting the session

Develop a routine where the children know that it is story time or poem/song time. Make sure children with sight or hearing disabilities are near to you and if possible, have adult support on hand for children with physical or learning difficulties.

Start with a simple rhythm or chant as a clear signal that it's time for stories or poems and songs, e.g. a clapping rhythm, word sounds or 'Time to sit, time to listen. 1-2-3 it's story time!'

Introducing the story or poem/song

It is important to engage the children's imagination and curiosity before you start telling your story or poem/song, e.g. a related prop such as baked bread for exploring senses; introducing a character image or puppet; using an image to encourage discussion or make up a small story about your own life that links to the story or poem/song theme.

Performance skills

A storyteller can use a range of different methods to tell a story or perform a poem or song to a young audience. These include:
- speaking slowly and clearly to a point behind the group so that all the children can hear you
- looking around the group while you perform so that every child feels involved
- using different voice tone to distinguish between different characters and their moods, as well as highlighting sound effects, actions and events
- using body actions to illustrate movements and expressions
- using a small number of props
- involving the children where possible, e.g. join in with actions, words, sounds
- improvising the text or actions if you can't remember the words or in response to the children's involvement or reactions
- positively acknowledging any interruptions and then weaving back to the story.
- revisiting the story or poem/song several times so that the children recognise it and join in with words and phrases.

The most important thing is to enjoy, share and have fun with the stories, poems and songs!

Theme: Being active

> **Learning outcomes**
>
> Children at the expected level of development will:
> - be confident to try new activities and show independence, resilience and perseverance in the face of challenge (ELG: Managing Self)

What you need:

- Our special story and rhyme basket/box' (optional)
- 'Star Jumpers Club – story
- Story board (optional)
- A Star Jumper card badge
- Photograph of children doing gymnastics or another activity
- 'Keeping active' body puppet – Resource sheet 1 (RS1)
- Our skeleton – Resource sheet 2 (RS2)

Getting ready:

Make the 'Star Jumpers' badge in advance by drawing a star or a child doing a star jump in the middle of the badge and attach a pin on the back. Have a photograph of children doing gymnastics or a physical activity and a Star Jumpers' badge available (or put it in 'Our special short story and rhyme box').

Introducing the story

Show the children the photograph and talk about the activity taking place. Highlight the importance of doing different physical activities to keep our bodies fit. (If you have children with physical disabilities, focus on what they can move – with or without support). Show the children the 'Star Jumpers badge' and explain it belongs to a girl called Amber who joins a gym club. Check that the children know what this is before reading or performing the story.

Performance suggestions

Use hands, arms and upper body to act out the different movements in the story. Slow down as you go through Joe and Amber's performance so that the children can follow each part of the exercise routine. Hold up the Star jumpers badge at the end of the story.

Ideas to reinforce theme

- Encourage the children to share their own experiences of doing physical activities of being part of a club, e.g. dance, gymnastics, football, swimming or a favourite playtime. Ask open questions to help the children talk more about the activity/sport such as why they like it, what they do and how it keeps them fit and healthy.

- Talk about how healthy bodies need to be active. Use the 'Keeping active body puppet – RS1'. Starting from the head, point to the main parts of the body and invite the children to say the names. Model gently stretching and moving each of your main body parts for the children to follow. Invite children to suggest an active song for the group to do, e.g. Head, shoulders, knees and toes, Hokey Cokey.

Consolidation activities

Game
Explore skeletons and how they are connected together to make our body frame. Display a full image of 'Our skeleton – RS2' to the children and name each section. Display a cut-up set of the bones and invite the children to help you build up another skeleton. Show the song *The Skeleton Dance* (found on YouTube) and encourage the children to join along and move the different parts of their bodies.

Role play
Encourage the children to try different actions performed in the story, e.g. bunny jumps, star jumpers, jumping upwards and down, different hops and ways to move around the room and in different directions. If suitable, suggest the children work in pairs or groups to perform a small routine.

Parachute game
Play a variety of active parachute games such as 'Merry-Go-Round' where the children hold the parachute in one hand and walk round (creating a merry-go-round). Change the movement to hopping, skipping or jumping as well as changing directions.

Star Jumpers Club

Amber and her Nan had come to see the Star Jumpers Club at their local sports centre.

Ever since the Star Jumpers Club had put on a show, Amber had wanted to be part of the group. She clapped and cheered as they jumped, hopped and skipped to the music or did forward rolls and handstands on a big mat. It looked like fun then but now she was not so sure. She didn't know anyone in the group and she suddenly felt very shy.

"I don't want to go in there!" Amber said to her Nan nervously. "Can we go home?"

Amber's Nan squeezed her hand gently. "Give it a go," she said. "If you don't like it, you don't have to come back next week."

Amber walked over to a group of children who were getting ready. She smiled at them but they were too busy putting on their gym shoes to notice her standing there.

Suddenly she heard a friendly voice.

"Hello. Are you alright?"

Amber looked round to see a boy smiling at her.

"My name's Joe," he said. "What's yours?"

"Amber," she said shyly.

"Welcome to the Star Jumpers Club," he grinned. "It's great fun here and there's lots to do and learn."

"Warm up time," called out their teacher. "Quickly find a space."

"What's a 'warm up'? Amber asked Joe.

"It's when we do some gentle exercises to stretch our muscles and get our bodies warmed up and ready to go for the rest of the lesson's activities." he replied.

Amber carefully watched and followed the teacher and Joe as they rolled their shoulders and arms, stretched out their legs and touched their toes. Her body felt better already!

Once they were warmed up, Joe showed Amber lots of different jumps – little jumps, bunny jumps, tuck jumps, jumps in and out of hoops and Amber's favourite jump – the star jump.

Using storytelling to talk about...**Health & Self care**

Star Jumpers Club

Then the teacher showed them how to do a forward roll followed by a tall stretch at the end. It was great fun.

"Let's make up a dance with all the moves we have learnt today," suggested Joe.

"OK," said Amber. "As long as there are star jumps in it!"

They found a space in the hall and worked together on their dance. Their teacher was so impressed with what they were doing, she asked Joe and Amber to perform it to the rest of the group.

First, they started skipping in a big circle.

Then they ran forwards, backwards and sideways all over the hall.

Next, Amber did some high star jumps while Joe did some tuck jumps.

Finally, they ended their dance with two perfect forward rolls and a tall stretch with their arms straight up in the air.

Everyone in the group clapped and cheered.

"Well done Amber and Joe!" exclaimed the teacher. "I think Amber deserves to wear our special Star Jumper's badge. Don't you, Star Jumpers?"

"Yes!" cheered everyone. Amber could not stop smiling.

Soon the lesson was over and it was time to go home.

"Bye Amber," said Joe. "See you next week."

"Well?" said Amber's Nan. "Do you want to come back next week?"

"Of course I do, Nan," laughed Amber, looking at her new badge, "I'm one of the Star Jumpers now!"

Related activities within the learning environment

Literacy

Leave out sets of handwriting patterns or letter/word formation cards to help children develop hand/eye co-ordination for writing skills. Encourage them to trace over the patterns/letters and then attempt to form their own.

Work with pairs or groups of children to identify and recognise initial letters sounds for different action verbs, e.g. hop, jump, kick, roll, run, catch. Leave out letters for them to select for each word. Older children could write out the letters to spell the complete words.

Mathematics

Ask the children to do a jump ten times. Count out loud with them. Change the jump and count another ten. The counting can be extended beyond ten and the activities can be changed; for example, to catching and throwing a ball.

Art & Craft

Leave out card circles for the children to make a badge or medal that shows their favourite physical activity. They could draw and colour in their own pictures or use images from the computer or in magazines that show the activity. Attach safety pins on back or ribbons to make it a medal.

Give each child a 'Keeping active' body puppet – RS1' copied onto card. Encourage them to attach the body parts together (with support, if needed) and then decorate/colour it for the activity of their choice. Let them use the puppets for imaginary role play.

Exploring

Enlarge 'Our skeleton – RS2' onto card and cut them out. Lay out the parts on the floor or on a table for the children to put the bones into the correct order. Have a copy of the skeleton nearby for their reference.

Have a messy play where children can explore the movements of their hands, fingers, toes and feet with different textures and mediums, e.g. sand, mud, water, paint etc.

Games

Leave out a range of different sized soft balls for the children to play with outside. Either organise a game such as roll and catch or allow the children to use their own ideas to create a game.

Layout out an indoor obstacle course using large soft building blocks and tunnels for the children to explore and use their bodies to move across.

Resource sheet 1

Keeping active body puppet

Copy onto card and cut out the parts.

Attach each section using split pins.

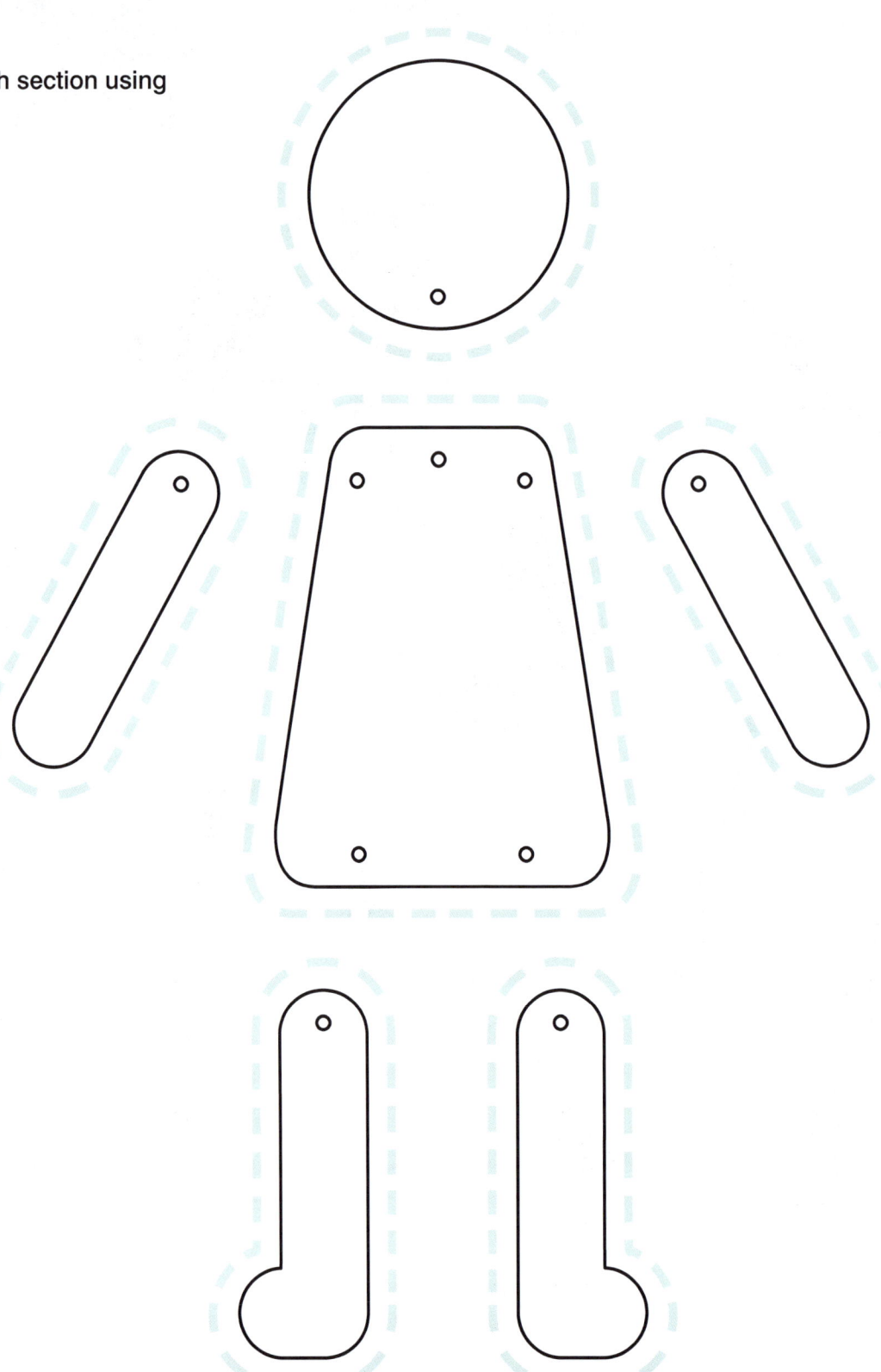

Keeping active body puppet

Using storytelling to talk about…**Health & Self care**

Resource sheet 2

Our skeleton

Use as a reference sheet or copy onto card and cut out the different bones to make up a new model skeleton.

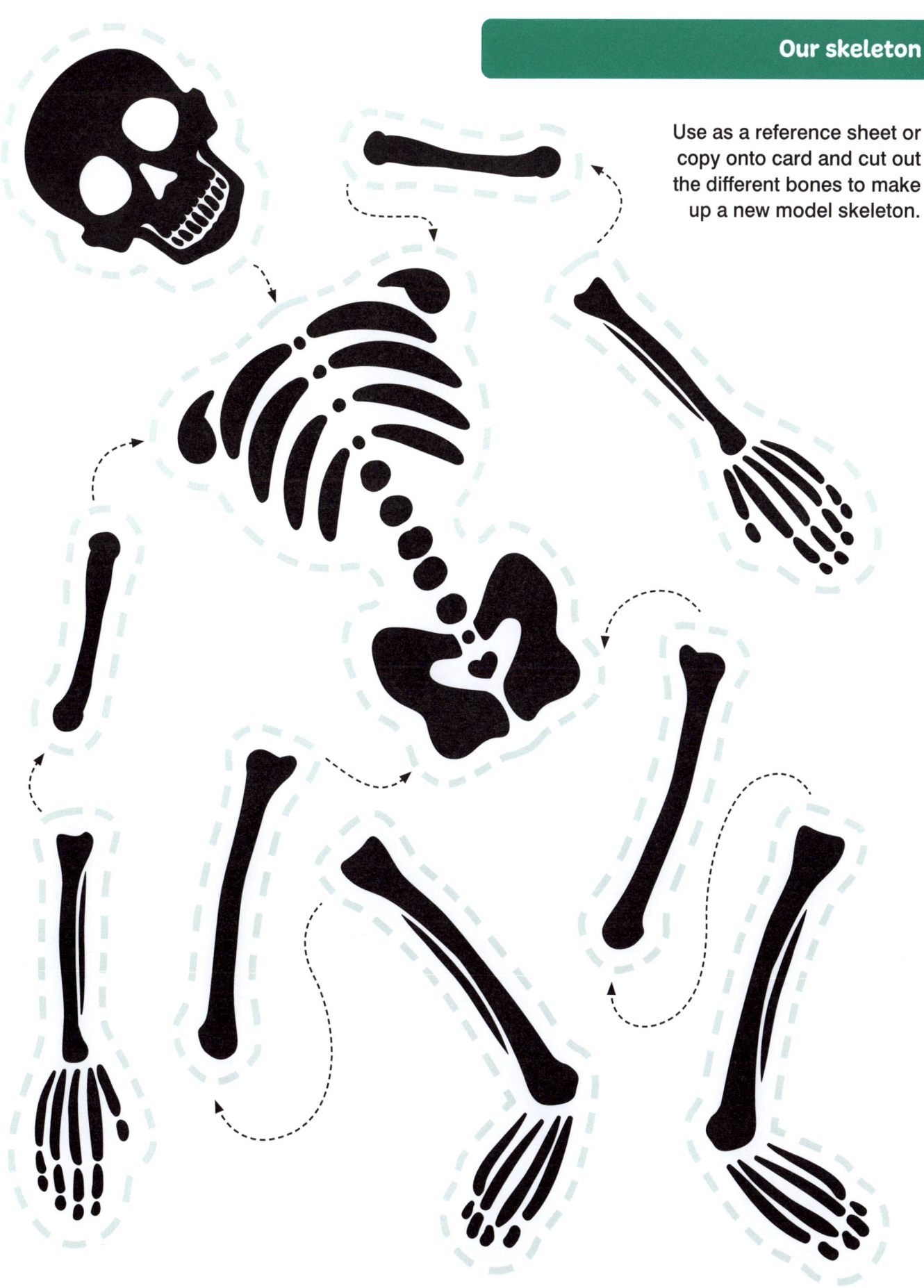

Using storytelling to talk about...**Health & Self care**

Theme: Different foods

Learning outcomes

Children at the expected level of development will:
- understand the importance of healthy food choices (ELG: Managing Self)

What you need:

- Our special story and rhyme basket/box' (optional)
- At the Market – song
- Story board (optional)
- Orange
- Images of the different foods in the poem (optional)
- 'Food market photograph – Resource sheet 1 (RS1)
- Food stall template – Resource sheet 2 (RS2)
- 'Making a sandwich' cards – Resource sheet 3 (RS3)

Getting ready:

Have a copy of 'Food market photograph – RS1 and an orange available (or put it in 'Our special short story and rhyme box'). If possible, collect images of the different foods mentioned in the song.

Introducing the song

This poem highlights the different types of food people could buy at a food market. The list of food is mostly healthy and multi-ethnic. Display or hold up the 'Food market photograph – RS1' for the children to see. Discuss where the picture is taken. Show the orange and say how all sorts of food can be bought at the market – some to eat straight away and some to cook with at home.
Display and name the different foods in the song (optional). Ask them listen to the different foods in your song.

Performance suggestions

This rhyming song is sung to the tune of 'Frère Jacques'. Sing it through once and then perform it again with the children joining in with the first two repeated lines.

Ideas to reinforce theme

- Use the song to discuss the different types of food as well as encouraging the children to share their ideas and experiences of the food., e.g. *Who has had a baked potato? What did you have as a filling? What fruits could you put in a take-away bowl of fruit salad? Which food would you want to eat? Why?*

- Show the children some examples of healthy food songs sourced on the Internet, e.g. *Vegetable soup* & *The Fruit Song* (The Singing Walrus). Encourage them to join in and sing along. Discuss how foods such as fruit and vegetables are good for our bodies and help them grow strong.

Consolidation activities

Performance

Split the children into pairs (18 food types) and give them a food each from the song, e.g. hot noodles, baked potatoes, fish and chips. Each verse has three types of food. Put each food pair into their verse group. Stand them in their correct food and verse order and encourage them to sing their food when signalled by you during the song.

Role play

Split the children into two groups. Ask one group to sell take-away food in a market and another group to buy the food. Encourage the children to ask for different types of food and the amount they want.

Circle game

Ask the children to think of one dish or food they would like to bring to a summer picnic (if possible try to exclude sweets or crisps). Start by modelling the sentence, '*For the picnic, I will bring an apple...*' Let the next child add to the list until everyone has contributed. Mime eating the picnic with the child.

Display

Create a food market place using all the children's market stall picture collages (see Art & Craft). Encourage them to write their names above the stall and add labels to show what food is sold in each one. Older children could write their own captions.

At the Market

(Sing to the tune of 'Frère Jacques')

      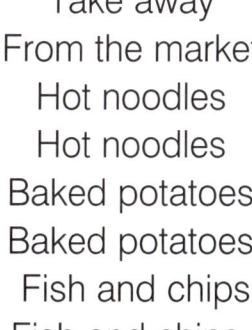 

Take away
From the market
Hot noodles
Hot noodles
Baked potatoes
Baked potatoes
Fish and chips
Fish and chips.

Take away
From the market
Fruit kebabs
Fruit kebabs
Crispy samosas
Crispy samosas
Sandwiches
Sandwiches.

Take away
From the market
Mushroom soup
Mushroom soup
Slice of pizza
Slice of pizza
Chicken wings
Chicken wings.

Take away
From the market
Fish stir fry
Fish stir fry
Curry and rice
Curry and rice
Oranges
Oranges.

Take away
From the market
Soft ice cream
Soft ice cream
Watermelon
Watermelon
Warm muffins
Warm muffins.

     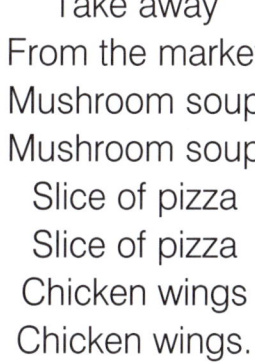         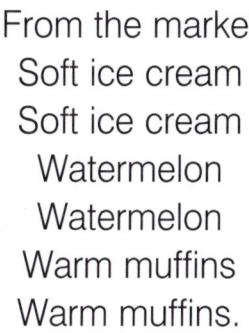       

Related activities within the learning environment

Literacy

Copy and laminate the 'Making sandwiches cards – RS3'. Cut them out and encourage pairs of children to say and put them in the correct sequence order.

Ask the children to bring in recipes from home or pictures/photographs of their favourite food. Collect them all together to make a class book. A book on favourite fruit and vegetables could also be created.

Mathematics

Draw large circles to represent vegetable pizzas and cut them into equal slices. Encourage the children to place the slices together to make one whole pizza again. Ask them to count how many make one whole (do quarter slices etc).

Use pictures or real fruit or vegetables for guessing and weighing activities or counting how many need to go into a paper bag or basket.

Art & Craft

Give the children a paper plate and soft/salt dough or cut-out images to create a plate of healthy food they would like to eat or share with others.

Give each child a copy of 'Food stall template – RS2' and a wide selection of food images from the Internet or magazines. Ask them what their food stall sells and to find images to stick on their stall. Use the stalls for display.

Exploring

Make simple sandwiches or biscuits using different shaped cutters. Encourage the children to discuss the order of how they are made or baked. Let them decorate the sandwiches or biscuits afterwards.

Make fruit salad or vegetable salad/pizza. As the children work, explore the features and vocabulary of the different vegetables or fruits e.g. seeds, peel, skin, fruit, root etc.

Role play corner

Set up a small market stall or a couple of market stalls with play food or salt dough food made by the children. Include weighing scales, packaging and play money.

Resource sheet 1

Food market photograph

Using storytelling to talk about…**Health & Self care**

Resource sheet 2

Market stall template

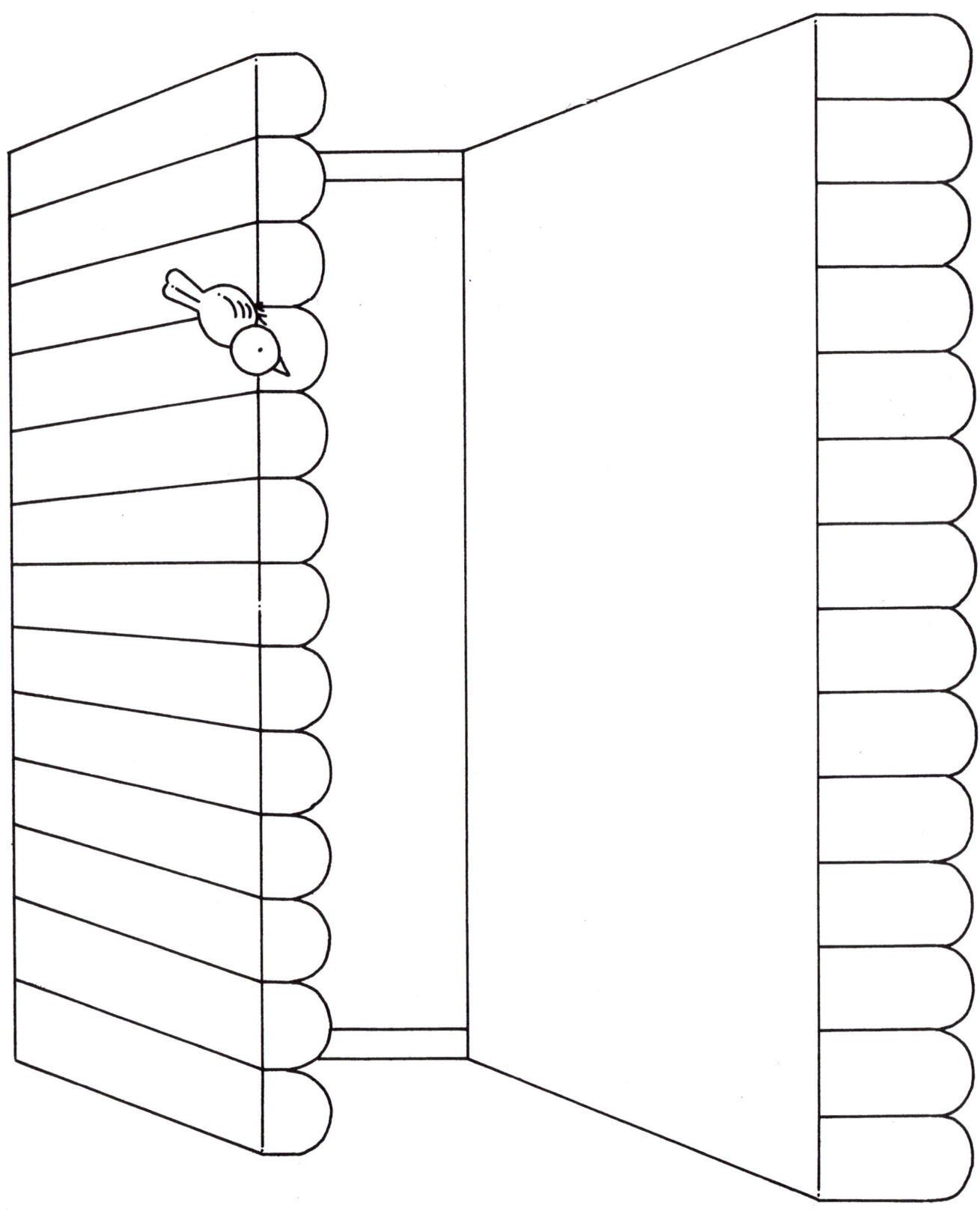

Resource sheet 3

'Making a sandwich' cards

Copy and cut out the pictures for sequencing and discussion activities.

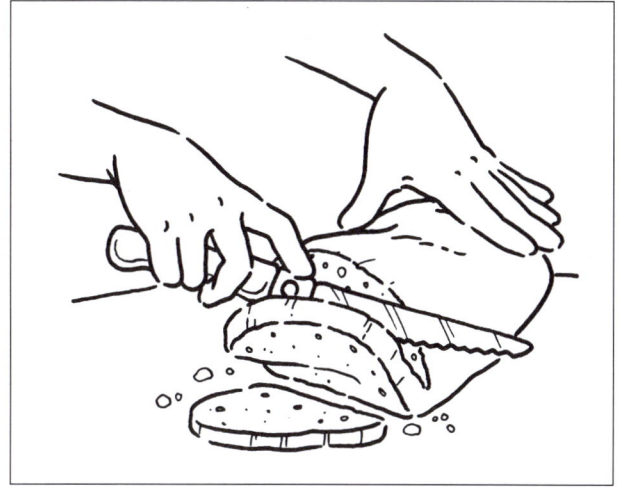
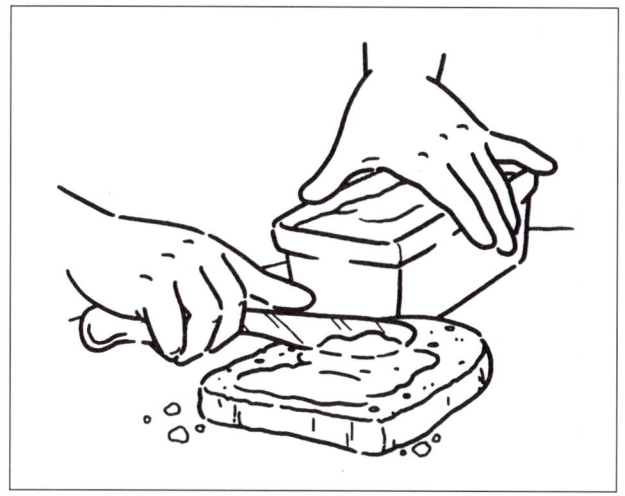
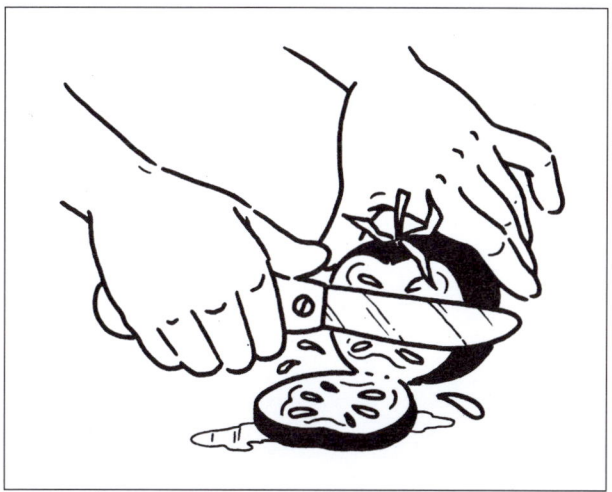

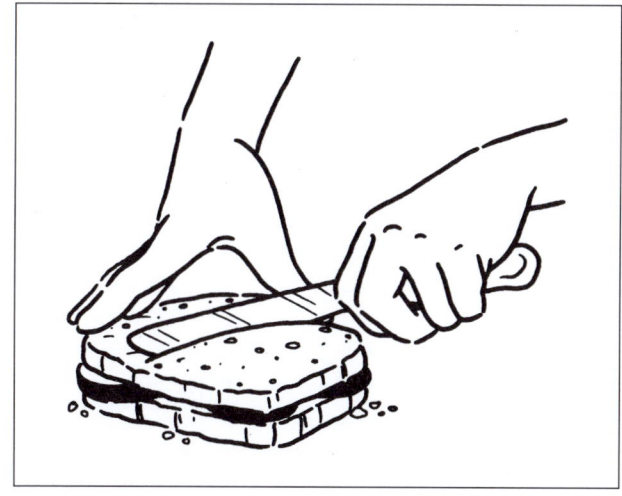

Using storytelling to talk about...**Health & Self care**

Theme: Keeping safe

Learning outcomes

Children at the expected level of development will:
- offer explanations for why things might happen… (ELG: Speaking)
- explain the reasons for rules, know right from wrong and try to behave accordingly (ELG: Managing Self)

What you need:

- Our special story and rhyme basket/box' (optional)
- Zig Gets Lost – story
- Story board (optional)
- Zig story characters – Resource sheet 1 (RS1)
- Zig story pictures – Resource sheet 2 (RS2)
- Zig's story map – Resource sheet 3 (RS3)
- Lost at the shops – Resources sheet 4 (RS4)

Getting ready:

Have the Zig character picture or puppet from 'Zig story characters– RS1 and the Zig's story map – RS3 available (or put it in 'Our special short story and rhyme box'). Have the other story characters and pictures from 'Zig story characters -RS1' and 'Zig story pictures – RS2' available if you want to show or use them while reading or performing the story.

Introducing the story

Show the children the picture/puppet of Zig the Alien. Explain that Zig is very excited as he is going to a fairground with his mum and dad on the Planet Zap. Show the Zig fairground story map to the children and point and name each part. Display on the storyboard with Zig and his parents.

Performance suggestions

It is important not to worry the children about Zig getting lost. Read the story in a calm voice so as not to worry the children about Zig getting lost. You may want to add the pictures to the story board or hold up each character or story picture as you tell the story.

Ideas to reinforce theme

The story 'Zig gets lost' focuses on straightforward actions a young child could take if they got lost. We recommend you ask advice from experts such as the police, if you want to have a discussion about the possible dangers of talking or going off with strangers.

- Use the characters, pictures and story map to help you discuss what happened in the story and what actions Zig took to help him find his parents again. Ask: *What did he do first? (He stayed where he was), What did he do next? (He asked the moon buggy alien to fetch the three-eyed alien in charge of missing persons.) What lesson did Zig learn? (not to wander off, and ask someone you trust for help).*

- Enlarge the pictures from the 'Lost at the shops – RS4' story and with the children, look and discuss what happens. Highlight that if they are lost, they should stay where they are and get an adult to find who could be trusted, e.g. a police officer. Discuss how Zig could have given his name and his mum's name.

Consolidation activities

Puppets
Use a Zig stick puppet or a class puppet and create a scenario where it has become lost. Encourage the children to ask it questions and help it find its parents or carers again. Model it saying its name and simple address.

Role play
Put the children into groups of three. Choose one child to pretend to be lost in a scenario that they would be familiar with, like a supermarket or shopping centre. Another child could be the shopkeeper who gets a police officer, and the last child could be the police officer. Watch the children closely and ask them what is happening as they play out the situation.

Display ideas
Create a large model of the Planet Zag's fairground (use 'Zig's story map – RS3' as a layout guide). Invite the children to draw the moon buggies, bouncy space rocket, UFO roller coaster plus any other stalls or rides. Stick small squares of Velcro on each area and onto the back of the Zig story characters. Move characters around the display and ask the children what Zig needs to do to find his parents. Do this several times.

zig gets lost

Zig the alien was at the big fair on Planet Zag. There were lots of great rides, like the UFO roller coaster, a bouncy space rocket and moon buggies that you could drive around a race track.

"Please can I go on all the rides, Dad?" asked Zig.

"We'll see," answered his dad. "What's more important is that you don't wander off on your own. There are a lot of aliens here today."

Zig looked around him. His dad was right, there were aliens everywhere!

"What if I get lost?" said Zig sounding worried. "How will I find you?"

Zig's mum smiled. "Well, if you get lost, remember to stay where you are and ask someone to get one of the three-eyed aliens who help with the fair."

After a while, Zig's mum and dad decided to buy some moon buns. Zig could see the moon buggies and really wanted to drive one around the race track.

"I'll just have a quick go on a moon buggy," he thought. "I'll only be a few minutes. Mum and Dad won't even notice I'm gone."

He ran over to the moon buggies and raced one round and round the race track.

After a while he stopped and looked for his mum and dad, but all he could see were lots of aliens he did not know.

"Oh no!" cried Zig. "Where are my mum and dad?"
Suddenly Zig remembered what his mum had said – "Stay where you are!"

Zig sat down by his moon buggy and waited for his mum and dad. But they didn't come.

"How am I going to find my mum and dad?" he cried.

An alien looking after the moon buggies came over to Zig.

"Are you alright?" she asked.

zig gets lost

"I've lost my mum and dad," Zig replied unhappily. "Can you ask one of the three-eyed aliens to find them for me?"

The moon buggy alien went off to a big tent. Soon she came back with one of the three-eyed aliens.

"What's your name?" the three-eyed alien asked Zig.

"Zig," he answered. "I've lost my mum and dad."

The three-eyed alien got out a special telephone and talked into it.

Suddenly, Zig heard a voice coming out of a large speaker above him.

"Attention!" it said. "We've found a little alien called Zig. Will his mum and dad please come to get him from the moon buggy race track?"

A few minutes later Zig heard voices that he knew well.

"Zig!" cried his mum. "Thank goodness you're safe."

Zig's dad looked very cross.

"Well, Zig?" he said. "We told you not to wander off on your own."

"Sorry, Dad," said Zig, and he burst into tears.

" But…" smiled his dad, "…we're very pleased that you stayed where you were and got help."

"Come on, Zig," said his mum gently. "I think you've had enough excitement for today. How about a moon bun?"

"Yes, please," said Zig wiping away his tears. "I'm starving!"

Related activities within the learning environment

Literacy

Encourage the children to write their full name. Think of different ways to decorate the names. Some children will also be able to write their address.

Select picture books on the theme of getting lost. Encourage the children to share the books with each other and discuss what happens to the characters in the stories.

Mathematics

Ask the children if they know their house or flat number. Look at each number and discuss how they would say it– 26 should be said 'twenty six' not 'two six'. Encourage more able children to think of numbers that come before or after their house number.

Art & Craft

Draw a maze outline on a card. Let the children stick small bricks or cards along the wall edges. Encourage them to try drawing their own mazes.

To help the children practise describing their parents and carers to other people such as the police, encourage them to draw their parents'/carers' faces. Label the drawings and put them on display.

Small world

Set out play sets for settings such as circuses, fairs and shops that attract large crowds. Encourage the children to role play scenarios where a character gets lost.

Games

Use copies of the 'Zig's story map – RS3' to play I-Spy games or a telling and following instructions game.

Role play corner

Set up a shop area where the children can role play being lost at the shops. Put out telephones for the children to use to call the police, parents or carers.

Resource sheet 1

Zig story characters

Cut out pictures and display on a storyboard or attach sticks for the children to see or hold up.

Zig

Mum

Dad

Moon buggy alien

Three-eyed alien

Using storytelling to talk about...**Health & Self care**

Resource sheet 2

Zig story pictures

Cut out pictures and display on a storyboard or attach sticks for the children to see or hold up.

Using storytelling to talk about…**Health & Self care**

Resource sheet 3

Zig's story map

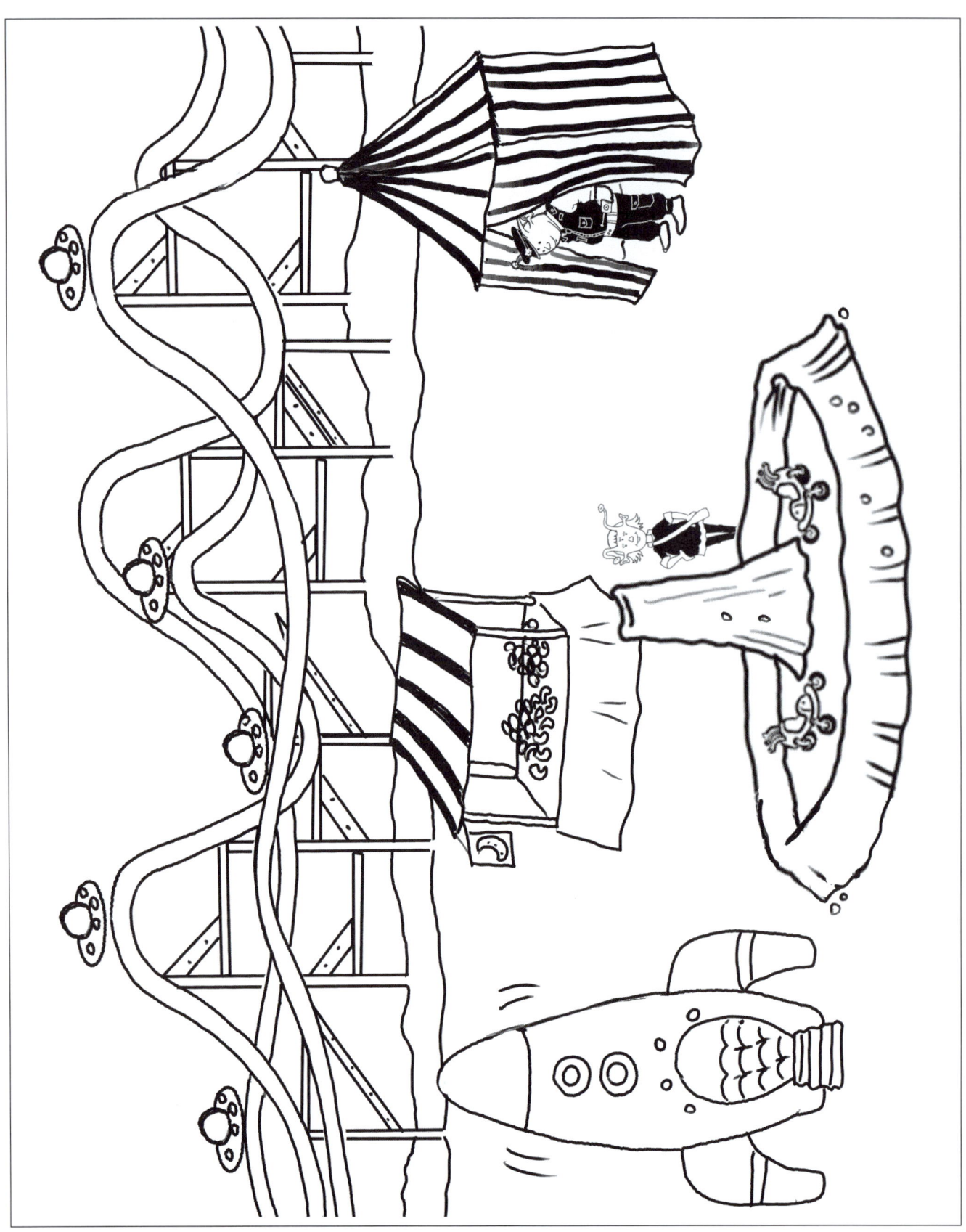

Using storytelling to talk about...**Health & Self care**

Resource sheet 4

Lost at the shops

Theme: Getting clean

Learning outcomes

Children at the expected level of development will:
- manage their own basic hygiene and personal needs, including dressing, going to the toilet. (ELG: Managing Self)

What you need:

- Our special story and rhyme basket/box' (optional)
- 'What Shall I do?' – song
- Soap, flannel (optional), towel and a small bowl of water
- Story board (optional)
- 'Dirty hands' photograph – Resource sheet 1 (RS1)
- 'What shall I do?' cards – Resource sheet 2 (RS2)
- 'What's in the bathroom?' – Resource sheet 3 (RS3)

Getting ready:

Have a copy of 'Dirty hands photograph – RS1' available (or put it in 'Our special short story and rhyme box'). Have soap, flannel, towel and small bowl of water near you. Copy and cut out 'What shall I do? cards – RS2' to display on the story board or to hold up.

Introducing the song

Show the children the 'Dirty hands photograph – RS1'. Point to the child's dirty hands. Ask: *What does the child need to do to get clean hands?*. Show the children the soap, flannel and towel. Invite them to go through a washing sequence with you – wet hands, use soap (flannel if needed), rinse hands, dry them with towel. Explain to the children that they are going to learn an action song about different ways they can get clean.

Performance suggestions

This is an action song sung to the tune of *'What shall I do with the drunken sailor'*. We have made some action suggestions alongside the song. Practise the song and actions before you perform it to the children. Perform it a couple of times so that the children feel confident joining with you.

Ideas to reinforce theme

Please note that the song 'Our Teeth' (p37) will go into more depth about caring for teeth.

- Use the 'What shall I do? cards – RS2' to show illustrations of the four messy and matching cleaning actions in the song. Display or hold up a pair and sing the relevant verse, with the children, e.g. muddy hands/soap and water. Ask questions about the actions, e.g. *How did the boy get muddy hands? How did he wash his hands?* etc.

- Use the 'What shall I do? cards – RS2' and the song to encourage children to share their own knowledge of washing and why it is important. Ask questions such as: *Why do we need to wash our hands before we eat? Why should we wash our hands after going to the toilet? Why do we wash when we wake up and go to bed?* If suitable, discuss why we wash ourselves, e.g. get rid of germs, stop skin getting itchy etc.

Consolidation activities

Role play
Read out instructions on how to wash hands for the children to follow and act out using sound effects for water (splash), e.g. Put the plug in the hole, turn on the taps, fill the bowl with warm water, dip your hands in the water, rub soap all over your hands and fingers, wash off the soap in the water until all the dirt is off, pull out the plug and dry your hands with a towel.

Performance
Put children into groups to perform the song. Split the children into two groups – one performing the messy question verses and the other group performing the washing answer verses. Another idea is to have eight groups with each group performing one of the verses.

Display
Create a display showing a photographic or pictorial sequence of how to wash hands and faces. The children could contribute their own pictures or take photographs of the children doing the sequence. Add simple captions underneath each part of the sequence.

What shall I do?

(Sing to the tune of 'What shall we do with the drunken sailor?')

What shall I do when my hands get muddy? What shall I do when my hands get muddy? What shall I do when my hands get muddy? Playing in the garden?	*(Point to each hand.)* *(Mime digging in the garden.)*
Wash your hands with soap and water. Wash your hands with soap and water. Wash your hands with soap and water. Then they won't be muddy.	*(Pretend to wash your hands with soap and water.)* *(Hold up clean hands.)*
What shall I do when my feet get sandy? What shall I do when my feet get sandy? What shall I do when my feet get sandy? Playing in the sand pit?	*(Point to your feet.)* *(Mime jumping in the sand pit.)*
Put them in the bath and wash the sand off. Put them in the bath and wash the sand off. Put them in the bath and wash the sand off. Then they won't be sandy.	*(Pretend to wash feet in the bath.)* *(Lift up clean feet.)*
What shall I do when my face gets dirty? What shall I do when my face gets dirty? What shall I do when my face gets dirty? Playing with the face paints?	*(Point to your face.)* *(Mime putting on face paint.)*
Wash your face with a warm, wet flannel. Wash your face with a warm, wet flannel. Wash your face with a warm, wet flannel. Then it won't be dirty.	*(Pretend to wash face with a flannel.)* *(Give a big smile for a clean face.)*
What shall I do when my teeth get sticky? What shall I do when my teeth get sticky? What shall I do when my teeth get sticky? Eating chewy sweeties?	*(Point to teeth.)* *(Mime chewing sticky sweets.)*
Brush them with a good clean toothbrush. Brush them with a good clean toothbrush. Brush them with a good clean toothbrush. Then they won't be sticky.	*(Pretend to brush your teeth.)* *(Show your teeth.)*

Using storytelling to talk about...**Health & Self care**

Related activities within the learning environment

Literacy

Ask the children to think up fun words or rhymes to describe washing like, 'scrub-a-dub-dub'. Share them with the class or group.

Record the song with the children. Have it available for them to listen to and join in. Have laminated 'What shall I do? Cards – RS2' available for them to put in the correct sequence.

Mathematics

Let the children draw round both hands and then use them for number writing (1–10), addition and subtraction activities. Include toes to make the total number of digits – 1-20.

Explore a sense of time and use time mathematical language by setting up a hand washing activity where you ask the children to soap and then rinse their hands for a set time (counting out loud).

Art & Craft

Give the children some soft (non-perfumed) soap and moulding/carving tools to create their own soap sculptures. If needed, offer suggestions such as animal shapes.

Have a fun hand and foot painting session where the children can add paint to their feet and hands to make their own pictures or work together to make a large group picture.

Games

Give each child or pairs a copy of 'What's in the bathroom? – RS3'. Ask them to find and mark eight dirty objects in the picture that don't belong in the bathroom, (spade, fork, snail, paint pots, boots, bicycle, teapot, saucepan). Discuss what other things are in the bathroom that would help them get clean.

Music

Sing more action songs relating to getting clean, e.g. 'This is the way we wash our hands' (sung to 'Here we go round the Mulberry Bush').

Exploring

Use a water play session to encourage children to investigate the textures and uses of a range of different bath sponges, flannels and wash brushes. Leave out dirty items for them to wash.

Have messy play sessions using a range of messy materials such as a gloop, wet sand and mud etc. Encourage or help the children to wash off the mess at the end of the activity.

Resource sheet 1

'Dirty hands' photograph

Using storytelling to talk about…**Health & Self care**

Resource sheet 2

'What shall I do?' cards

Copy and cut out each image for discussion, matching and game activities.

Resource sheet 3

What's in the bathroom?

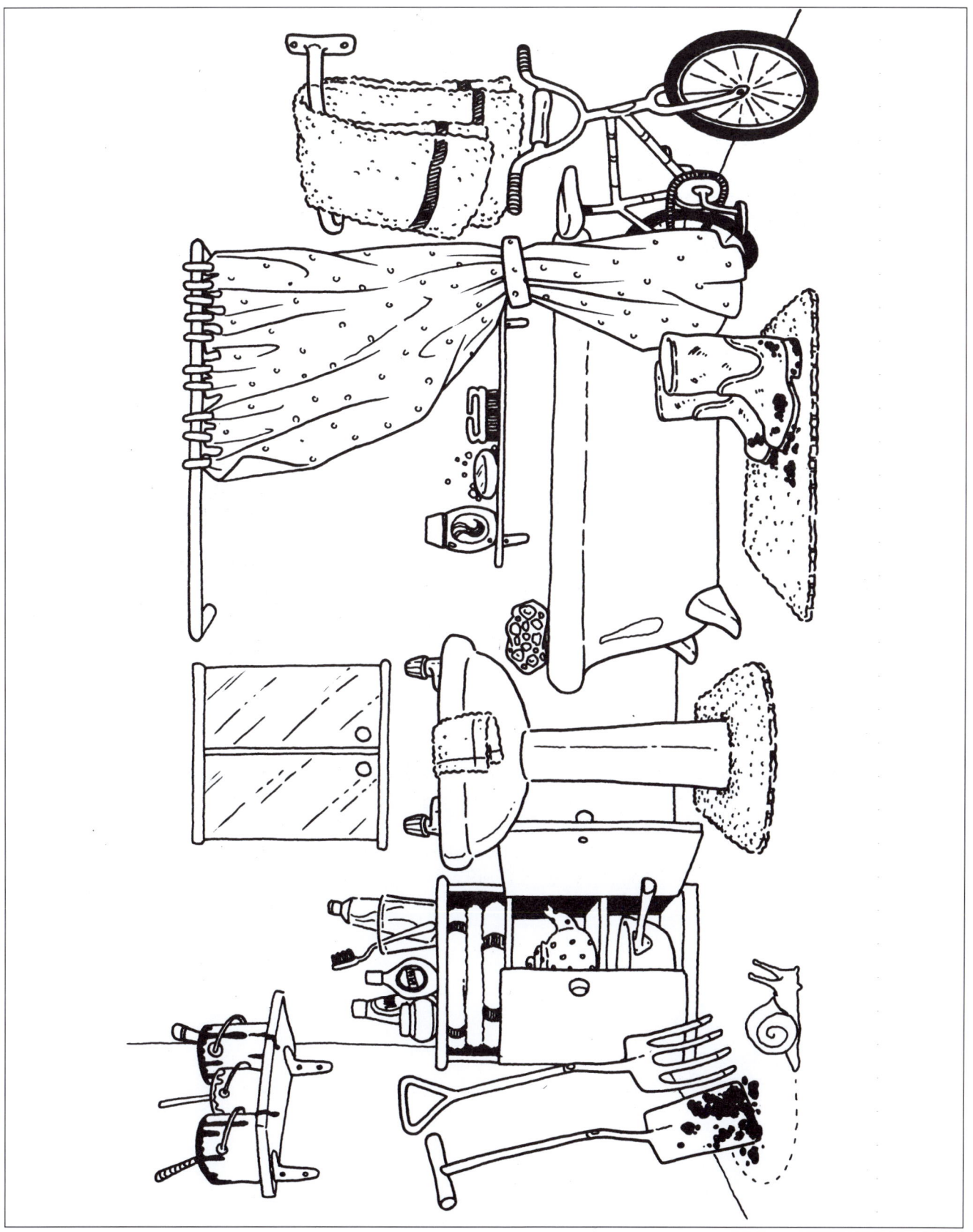

Using storytelling to talk about...**Health & Self care**

Theme: Using a hankie

Learning outcomes

Children at the expected level of development will:
- manage their own basic hygiene and personal needs, (Managing Self)
- show an understanding of their own feelings and those of others (ELG: Self-Regulation)

What you need:

- 'Our special story and rhyme basket/box' (optional)
- Snozzle the Sneezing Giant – song
- Story board (optional)
- Giant hankie (large patchwork style cloth)
- Hankie
- 'Snozzle the Sneezing Giant' picture – Resource sheet 1 (RS1)
- A giant hankie – Resource sheet 2 (RS2)

Getting ready:

Use 'Snozzle the Sneezing Giant – RS1' as a stick puppet or as a picture on the story board. Have a hankie available (or put it in 'Our special short story and rhyme box'). Make a giant hankie by using a large piece of patchwork style material or create one using fabric glue or stitching (try to use lots of patchwork colours and patterns). Create a basket of different pieces of cloth.

Introducing the story

Before you start the story, make sure the giant hankie is well hidden. Take out a hankie and sneeze into it. Explain that when we have a runny nose or need to sneeze, we should try and use a hankie so that we don't pass on germs. Introduce Snozzle and explain that he wasn't very good at using a hankie – start story.

Performance suggestions

Encourage the children to actively take part in this story. Let them join in with 'Bing a bong bong – wow!' rhyme, the song and the mime movements for the villagers. Place an emphasis on Snozzle's sneezing – make it loud but be aware of any noise sensitivity. Make a big event of revealing the giant hankie. Spend time looking at the different patterns and colours.

Ideas to reinforce theme

- Use the story to discuss using a hankie and spreading germs. Ask questions such as: *What did Snozzle do when he woke up? How did Snozzle wipe his nose? Why did the villagers start sneezing and catching colds? (Snozzle's sneezing spread his germs.) How did a hankie help Snozzle and everyone get better?*

Consolidation activities

Puppets
Make a giant Snozzle puppet and let the children use it to suggest other ways that Snozzle could have spread his germs and ways he could have avoided it.

Role play
Let the children pretend to be villagers at the meeting. Ask them to think of other ways to stop Snozzle sneezing. Encourage them to share their ideas with the group through acting or miming.

Circle game
Ask the children to imagine that they are helping to make a giant hankie out of lots of different pieces of material. Invite them to mime stitching all the materials together with you. Suggest sharing favourite stories, rhymes, news, favourite ideas or facts while stitching. Start the process. For children who are shy or nervous, ask open questions about what a child has been doing or highlight a skill or interest.

Ideas for display
Make a big picture of Snozzle the giant. Let the children help you decorate or paint him for the display. Next to Snozzle, put up the giant hankie made by the class in Art & Craft. Label the display to explain why Snozzle needs his hankie.

Snozzle the Sneezing Giant

Once upon a time there was a giant called Snozzle who lived on a big hill above a small village. Snozzle was a very kind and happy giant and the villagers in the valley loved hearing him sing a little song, which went like this –

'Bing a bong bong, Bing a bong bong, Bing a bong bong, Bing a bong bong – wow!'

One morning, Snozzle woke up, stretched his arms and began to sing his song

"Bing a bong bong, Bing a bong bong, Bing a bong bong, Bing a bong bong – Ahhhhh – tishoo!"

"Oh no!" sneezed Snozzle. "I think I've got a cold."

He wiped his nose with his hand (slurp) and plodded slowly into the kitchen to have his breakfast.

But he sneezed into his porridge (atishoo!), he sneezed onto toast (atishoo!) and he sneezed into his glass of milk (atishoo!).

"I don't like sneezing," sniffed Snozzle unhappily. "I'm going back to bed. Perhaps I will stop sneezing tomorrow (atishoo!)."

But Snozzle sneezed the next day and the next day and the next day! "Atishoo."

He could not stop sneezing!

"Ahhhhh – tishoo!"

Now the villagers at the bottom of the hill were also unhappy. Snozzle's sneezes were so strong that the leaves were blown off the trees and so loud that all the houses shook. To make matters worse, many of the villagers started sneezing too as Snozzle's germs spread around the village. At school the children could only play, 'Ring a ring a roses'! Let's pretend to be the children and sing it.

Ring a ring a roses
A pocket full of posies
Atishoo, atishoo
We all fall down.

The villagers decided to have a special meeting in the village hall to work out how they could stop Snozzle sneezing but no one could think of a good idea.

Then a little girl, called Maya, put up her hand.

"Excuse me," she said politely. "But what do we use when we sneeze?"

Snozzle the Sneezing Giant

"Our hand," called out one villager

"Our sleeves," cried out another.

"No, no, no!" exclaimed Maya. "We should use a hankie to wipe our noses."

"Of course," said the villagers.

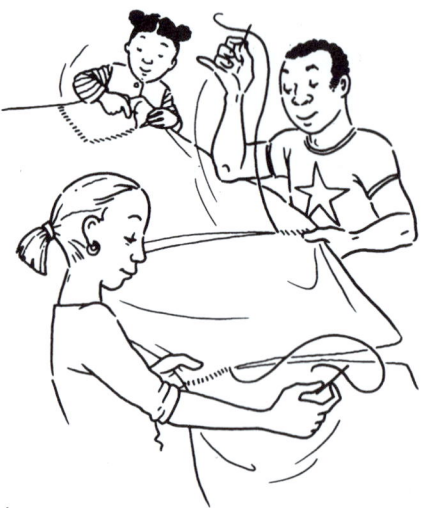

"So let's make Snozzle a giant hankie to wipe his germs away and not give others a nasty cold," suggested Maya.

Everybody thought it was a great idea. They all rushed home to find old sheets, tea towels, curtains, scarves and even table clothes. All day and all night, the villagers worked together in the village hall to cut and stitch the hankie together.

By the next morning, they had made a giant hankie made of many colours and patterns. Would you like to see it? (unravel your giant hankie and look at it in detail).

Suddenly they heard…

"Ahhhhh – tishoo!" Snozzle was awake!

The villagers quickly put the giant hankie on the back of a cart and pushed and shoved it up to Snozzle's house on the hill.

Knock! Knock!

"Atishoo! Who is there?" called out a big, sad voice. "I can't stop sneezing and my cold won't go away."

"It's the villagers, Snozzle!" Maya shouted. "We've brought something for your cold."

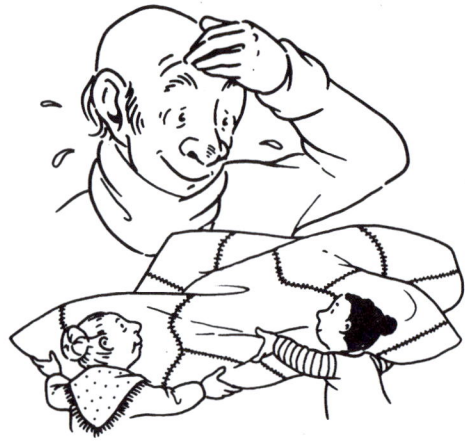

Snozzle slowly opened the door. He had a very sore, red nose and looked very fed up. The villagers held up the colourful hankie.

"What's that for?" sniffed Snozzle glumly.

"When you need to sneeze or wipe your nose," said Maya, "use this hankie to catch the nasty germs."

Snozzle thanked the villagers and took the hankie. After two or three days, Snozzle's cold went away and he had stopped sneezing. Instead the villagers heard a happy,

"Bing a bong bong, Bing a bong bong, Bing a bong bong, Bing a bong bong – wow!"

And now whenever Snozzle wants to sneeze he always uses his big colourful giant hankie.

Related activities within the learning environment

Literacy

Highlight the 'sn' sounds in 'Snozzle', 'sneeze' and 'sniff'. Ask the children to think of other words beginning with the 'sn' sound, like 'snake', 'snail', 'snip' and 'snore'.

Leave out folded cards and pencils/pens for the children to make 'Get well' cards for Snoozle or for someone they know. Write out the words in the cards for the children to trace over or encourage older children to sound out and write the words themselves.

Mathematics

Give copies of the 'A giant hankie – RS2' to each child to use to make patterns using two or three colours. They could create their own pattern and then swap the hankie with another child. They could also make patterns using shapes in the squares.

Use the 'A giant hankie – RS2' as a counting board for 3s or numbers from 1–12. Add counters to the squares for addition and subtraction skiils. Let the children use square shapes to make their own hankie (1–10 squares/ 15/20 squares).

Art & Craft

Give out copies of the 'A giant hankie – RS2'. Provide different coloured and textured paper and ask the children to stick different pieces of paper onto the different parts of the hankie to make their own hankie design.

Give out white squares of cloth. Using cloth paints or fabric pens let the children design a hankie as a gift to take home. Let them do another one and join each square together with fabric glue or ribbons to make a class giant hankie for Snozzle.

Music

Learn and sing songs relating to not being well or not spreading germs, e.g. Miss Polly had a dolly, 'Ring a ring a roses' and 'The Sneezing Song' (see YouTube).

Small world

Set out a town or village and figures for the children to re-enact the story.

Role play corner

Leave out a doctor's or nurse's kit for role-play. Toys could be used as patients.

Using storytelling to talk about…**Health & Self care**

Resource sheet 1

'Snozzle the Sneezing Giant' picture

Copy and cut out to use as a stick puppet or to be displayed on a storyboard.

'Snozzle the Sneezing Giant' picture

Resource sheet 2

A giant hankie

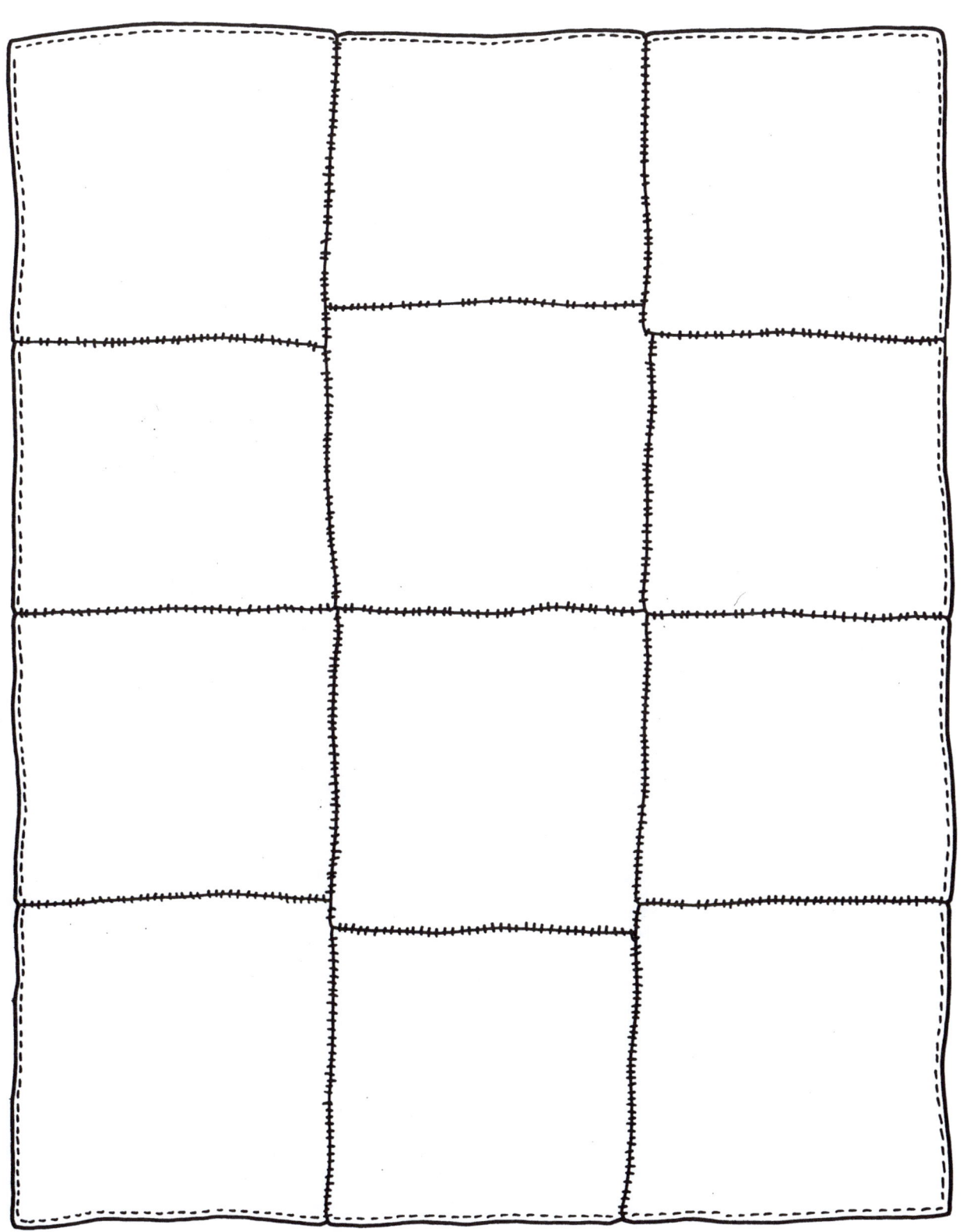

Theme: Caring for our teeth

Learning outcomes

Children at the expected level of development will:
- manage their own basic hygiene and personal needs, including dressing, going to the toilet. (ELG: Managing Self)

What you need:

- 'Our special story and rhyme basket/box' (optional)
- Our Teeth – poem
- Story board (optional)
- Toothpaste and toothbrush
- 'Our Teeth' cards – Resource sheet 1 (RS1)
- 'Cleaning my teeth' – Resource sheet 2 (RS2)
- 'Caring for my teeth'– Resource sheet 3 (RS3)

Getting ready:

Copy and cut out 'Our Teeth cards – RS1'. Attach each picture to sticks or display them in verse order on the storyboard. Have the toothpaste and toothbrush available (or put it in 'Our special short story and rhyme box').

Introducing the poem

Show the children your toothpaste and toothbrush. Encourage children to mime cleaning their teeth with you. Ask: *What important jobs do our teeth do for us?* Introduce the poem by pointing to the animal pictures on the storyboard or hold up the lion stick picture. Explain that teeth are important to animals too. Perform or read poem.

Performance suggestions

Use facial expressions and body movements to show the different teeth actions of the animals in the poem. Emphasise the underlined teeth action verbs. Point to yourself and sound upbeat when saying the last two verses. Reread the poem again with the children joining in with the repetitive phrase, 'a (animal) uses its teeth.

Ideas to reinforce theme

- Highlight how important it is for us to look after our teeth. Discuss how we should try to brush our teeth when we get up and before we go to bed. Encourage the children to share how they brush their teeth. Perform the sequence with the children while giving instructions on what to do.

- Show a film/video from the Internet about a child's first visit to the dentist or photographs of a dentist surgery. Encourage the children to share their own experiences of the dentist. Highlight the positive reasons of a visit.

Consolidation activities

Puppets

Use puppets to demonstrate ways to clean teeth, or a scene at the dentist. Encourage the children to re-enact the scenarios through the puppets. Leave them out for the children to explore different issues on healthy teeth.

Performance

Encourage the children to re-enact the poem. Take time to explore with the children how each animal moves and also uses its teeth. The whole class could perform each animal as you tell the poem or you could divide them into eight animal groups to perform their verse and then join together to do the human actions.

Game

Enlarge two copies of the teeth from 'Caring for my teeth – RS3' and cut them out. Draw a happy face on one and a sad face on another. Show images of good food/drink and bad food/drink for our teeth, e.g. a range of vegetables, certain fruits, water vs sweets, sugared drink, biscuits, cakes etc. Invite the children to help you place them by the correct tooth. Extend the activity by placing the teeth on the floor and giving images to the children to put on correct tooth. Discuss what could happen to teeth if we treat them badly.

Our Teeth

A lion uses its teeth
To cut its lunch in two.

A panda uses its teeth
To strip the thin bamboo.

A shark uses its teeth
To bite fish in the sea.

A beaver uses its teeth
To gnaw wood from a tree.

A crocodile uses its teeth
To snap at all who pass.

A cow uses its teeth
To munch the fresh, green grass.

A squirrel uses its teeth
To crunch nuts, hard as stone.

A dog uses its teeth
To chew a juicy bone.

And I use my teeth
In many different ways.

I like to keep them clean
By brushing twice a day.

Related activities within the learning environment

Literacy

Give each child a copy of 'Cleaning my teeth – RS2'. Cut out the pictures (or let them cut them out) and ask children to put them into the correct teeth cleaning sequence while explaining each action. Make zig-zag booklets for the children to stick the images into and create a front cover. Older children could write simple captions with each picture.

Mathematics

Create mouths with different amount of teeth (white stickers or cotton wool) in each one. The children could add more teeth or take them away. They could also put each mouth in order of how many teeth each one has.

Make a simple block chart with the children to show how many teeth different animals may have. Use it to encourage the children to use comparison language.

Art & Craft

Copy 'Caring for my teeth – RS3' onto card. Let the children decorate the toothbrush and toothpaste using colouring pens/paint or materials e.g. straw, wool for brush. Ask them to add a fun face to the tooth and write out their name on the tooth or under it.

Bend a paper plate in half to make a moving mouth. Let the children paint it red and add white teeth along the edge using white card, sponge painted white, or other materials.

Visitors & trips

Invite a dentist, dental hygienist or health visitor to talk to the group about looking after their teeth.

Small world

Set out small figures to play dentist visits and teeth cleaning routines at home.

Role play corner

Set up an area for the children to role play visiting the dentist.

Set up an area for the children to explore cleaning their teeth, with small basins, mirrors and toothbrushes. (They should not share toothbrushes.)

Resource sheet 1

'Our Teeth' cards

Resource sheet 2

Cleaning my teeth

Resource sheet 3

Caring for my teeth

Copy and cut out images for games, displays and activities.

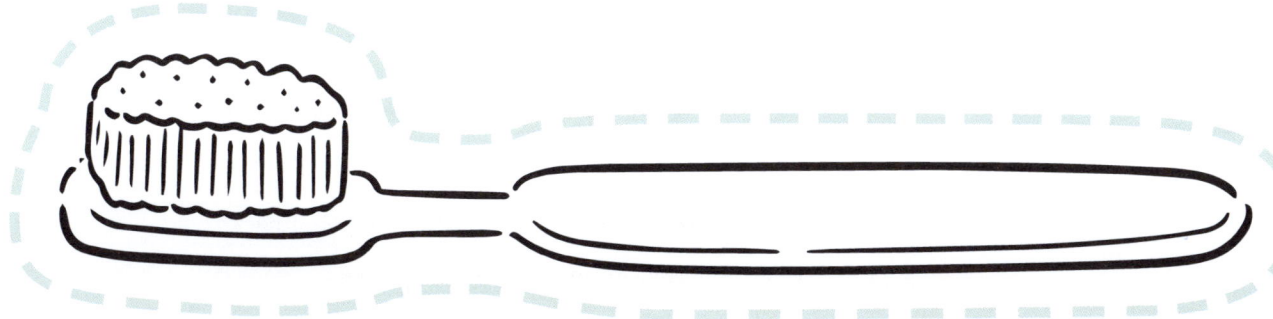

Theme: Dressing for the weather

Learning outcomes

Children at the expected level of development will:
- manage their own basic hygiene and personal needs, including dressing, going to the toilet (ELG: Managing self)
- understand...changes in the natural world around them (ELG: The Natural World)

What you need:

- Our special story and rhyme basket/box' (optional)
- Changing weather – short action story
- Story board (optional)
- Rain hat, winter woolly hat, sun hat
- 'Changing weather' storyboard – Resource sheet 1 (RS1) and Resource sheet 2 (RS2)
- Weather signs templates – Resource sheet 3 (RS3)

Getting ready:

Have the hats available (or put it in 'Our special short story and rhyme box'). If needed, copy and colour the three weather signs (sun, raindrop, snowflake) from 'Weather signs template – RS3'.

Introducing the story

Ask the children what the weather is like today. Model language such as 'Today it is cloudy'. Show the children the different hats. Ask: *Which hat could I wear for a hot day?* Do the same with the other hats. If using the weather signs, point to each one as you ask the questions. Explain that you are going to tell them a very active story about two children who kept having to put on different clothes because the weather kept changing.

Performance suggestions

This short story is very active and encourages the children to participate. It starts off slowly but should be speeded up so the children get a sense of the speed of the change of clothes. There should be a pause before the final part of the story. Encourage the children to join in with the repetitive text.

Ideas to reinforce theme

- Discuss what happened in the story. Ask questions such as, *What did Megan and JJ put on when it started to rain? What did they wear when it was warm outside? Why did they change into shorts, T-shirt and sun hat to play football in the sun? What did they put on when it started to get windy?*

- Have a discussion about what the children wear for different weather conditions. For example: *What kind of clothes do you wear when it is cold outside? Why? What kind of clothes do you wear when it is hot outside? Why?* (Highlight the need to wear a hat in hot sun.) *What are your favourite clothes in wintertime? What are your favourite clothes in summertime?*

Consolidation activities

Role play
Read the story aloud and ask the children to mime putting on or taking off the clothes. See if they can keep up with the speed of the story. Split the children into three groups. One group does the actions for the story, another group joins in with the repetitive text and the third group makes musical sounds to represent the change of weather.

Circle time
Put the children into a circle. Put a pile of hats (including rain hats, woolly hats and sun hats) in the middle of the circle. Ask a child to pick up a hat and mime something they could do while wearing that hat. The other children decide what it could be. The children could also do the actions in pairs.

Display
Display the collage pictures of types of clothes suitable for different weather (See Art & Craft) around the big cut-outs of a raindrop, a sun and a snowflake (use 'Weather signs template – RS3'). On a display table, lay out examples of clothing the children might wear for different seasons.

Changing Weather

JJ and Megan are staying at their aunt and uncle's house. After breakfast, JJ and Megan want to go and play in the garden. It is cold and cloudy.

They put on their gloves, jackets and hats.

They run outside and play hide and seek.

ONE, TWO, THREE – I'M COMING, READY OR NOT!

Suddenly, it starts to rain!

"Yuk!" says JJ. "I'm getting wet out here."

They run back inside and put on their raincoats and boots.

They run outside and jump in all the muddy puddles.

ONE, TWO, THREE – SPLASH!

Suddenly, the sun comes out and it stops raining.

"Hmmm," says Megan, "I'm getting warm out here."

They run inside and take off their coats and boots and put on their jumpers and trainers.

They run outside and have running races.

ONE, TWO, THREE – GO!

Suddenly, the sun starts shining very brightly.

"Phew!" says JJ. "I'm getting very hot out here."

They run inside and put on their shorts, t-shirts, sun-hats and sandals.

They run outside and play football.

ONE, TWO, THREE – GOAL!

Suddenly, it gets very windy.

"Whee!" says Megan. "I'm getting blown about out here."

They run inside and put on their trousers, jumpers and trainers.

They run outside and fly their kites.

ONE, TWO, THREE – UP!

Suddenly…

DRIP, DRIP, DRIP, DRIP, DRIP, DROP, DRIP, DROP,
DRIP DROP, DRIP DROP, DRIP DROP, DRIP DROP

"Oh, no," laugh JJ and Megan, "It's raining AGAIN!"

They run inside and…

…have lunch!

Using storytelling to talk about…**Health & Self care**

Related activities within the learning environment

Literacy

Write 's' in the sun and 'r' in the raindrop from 'Weather signs template - RS3'. Invite the children to say and add 's' and 'r' words (copy or draw images) to create mobiles.

Cut up copies of 'Changing weather' story – RS1 and RS2'. Let the children stick the images in the correct order into a small book and retell the story.

Mathematics

Put out sets of mixed up pairs of shoes and gloves. Ask the children to find the matching pairs. Highlight that things that come in twos can be called 'pairs'.

Over a period of time, help the children investigate different weather conditions, e.g. leave out measured containers outside when it is raining to see how much water goes into it, show how temperatures go up on temperature measuring equipment.

Art & Craft

Let the children make hot and cold clothing collage pictures using cut out pictures/photographs from the Internet or magazines etc. They could also use materials to cut out clothes shapes to dress a figure for a hot or cold day.

Help the children to make sun visors out of card. Use a long narrow strip to go round the head and a moon shape for the visor. Let the children decorate the visor.

Environment

During a wet week have a 'welly day'. Ask the children to bring in their wellies and let them enjoy splashing in puddles and walking on wet or muddy surfaces.

Games

Copy and cut out the pictures from 'Changing weather story – RS1 and RS2'. Ask the children to match the six weather pictures to the suitable clothes pictures the characters are putting on.

ICT

Find video examples on the Internet for the children to watch of EYFS level songs and games about using the correct clothing for different weather conditions.

Role play corner

Display outdoor clothing, hats and outfits that are mentioned in the story. Let the children dress up in the clothes and role play going out in different weathers.

Resource sheet 1

'Changing Weather' storyboard

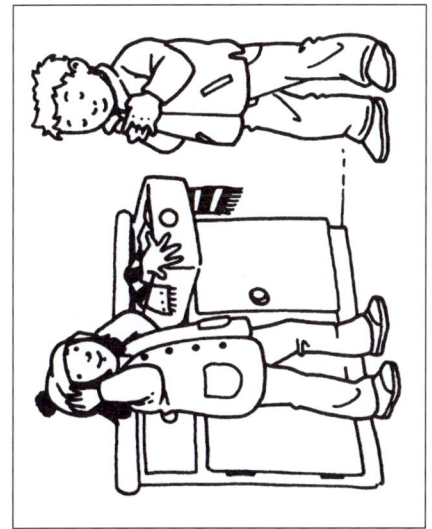
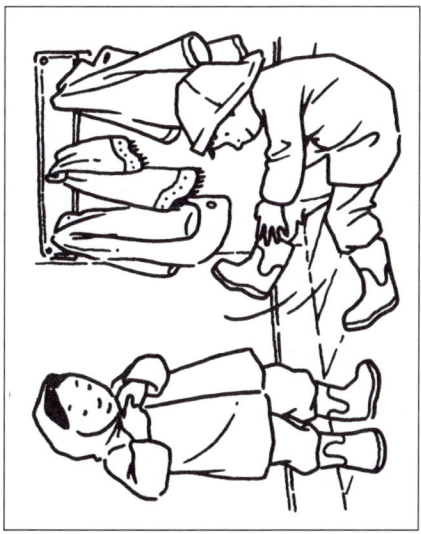

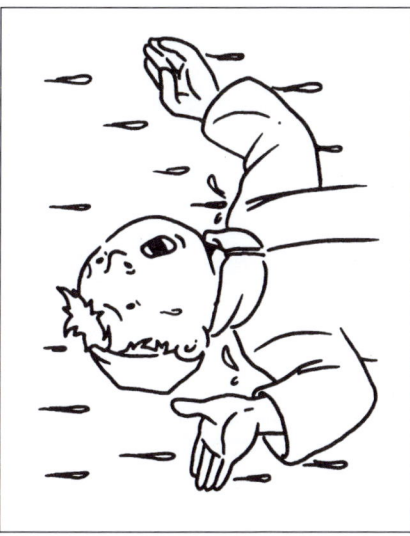
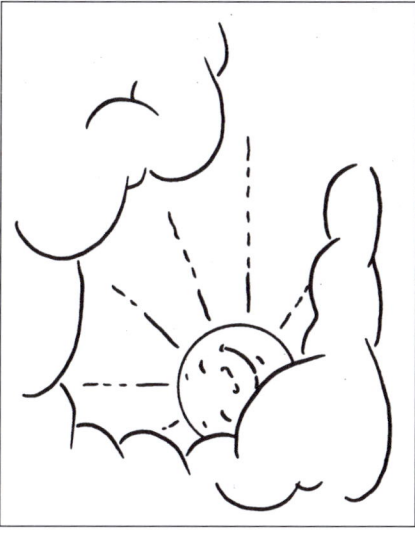

Resource sheet 2

'Changing Weather' storyboard

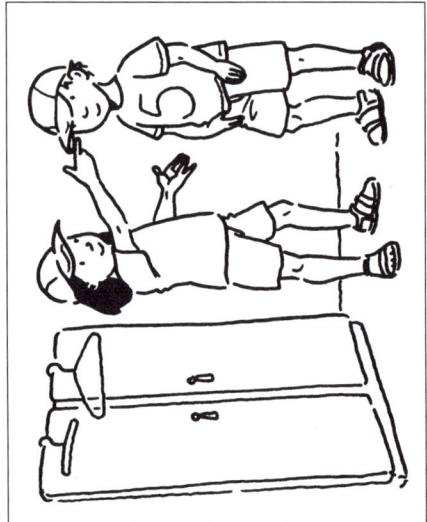
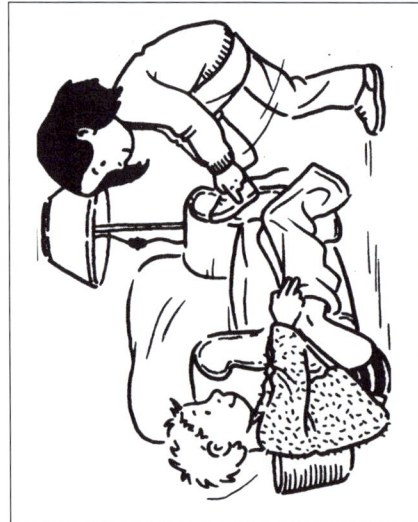

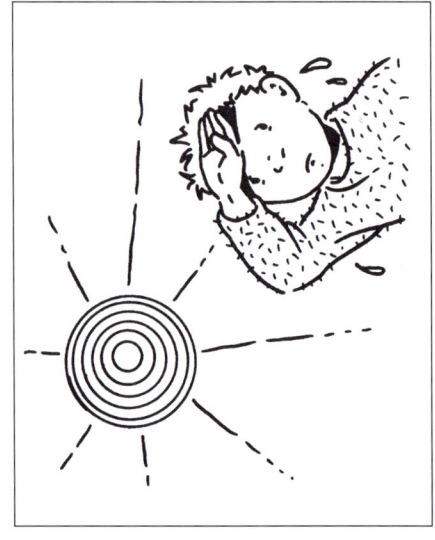

Resource sheet 2

Weather signs templates

Copy and cut out images for games, displays and activities.

Theme: Different clothes fastenings

Learning outcomes

Children at the expected level of development will:
- manage their own basic hygiene and personal needs, including dressing, going to the toilet. (ELG: Managing self)
- show an ability to follow instructions involving several ideas or actions (Self-Regulation)

What you need:

- 'Our special story and rhyme basket/box' (optional)
- All Done Up – poem
- Story board (optional)
- A top (coat or cardigan) with a zip
- Coat with a zip, shirt with buttons, belt with buckle, shoes with laces (optional)
- 'All Done up' pictures – Resource sheet 1 (RS1)
- 'How to do it' poster – Resource sheet 2 (RS2)
- Which is the right one? – Resource 3 (RS3)

Getting ready:

Have the top available (or put it in 'Our special short story and rhyme box'). Copy and cut out the 'All Done Up pictures – RS1' to be either displayed on the storyboard or held up by sticks.

Introducing the poem

Put on the top and explain that you need to do it up using the zip or buttons. Invite them to give you advice or slowly talk through how you do it. Highlight that some fastenings, like buttons and laces, need time and practice. Show the four pictures of the children from the poem trying to use different fastenings and say each one, e.g. zip, buttons, belt buckle, shoe laces. Explain that you know a poem that will help the four children to use them.

Performance suggestions

As you read the poem, try to use hand movements to show the actions of using the fasteners or take time to learn the poem so that you model how to do up real fasteners on clothing as you say each verse. Encourage the children to join in with the repetitive phrases and action words.

Ideas to reinforce theme

- Ask questions to re-enforce how the four children in the poem worked out how to use the different fasteners. Use the poem, pictures and clothing props (if used) as support. For example: *How does Clara's coat do up? Let's remember how she used a zip (repeat the first two lines of 2nd verse), etc.*

- Focus on the four different fasteners in more detail and encourage the children to share their own skills and knowledge on how to use them. Use clothing props or display the 'How to do it poster – RS2' and refer to each image in turn. Ask questions such as: *Where can we often find zips? (clothes, shoes, sleeping bag, school bags etc). Let's go through the actions of doing up a zip. (Highlight the need to keep the zip straight and pull up slowly).*

Consolidation activities

Performance
Perform the poem with the children. Split the children into two groups. Let one group say the first two lines of a main verse, e.g. *'Clara, do your coat up, zip, zip, zip'* while the other group asks how to do it. You say do the instruction verse while all the children mime the action.

Circle game
Put the children into a circle. Have a set of clothing/belts/shoes in the middle of the circle that uses different fastenings, e.g. laces, zips, buttons, buckles. Use clapping rhythms to go round the circle. Stop at a child or a pair of children and ask them to choose something from the middle. They can either show how the fastener works or ask the group how it's done. Continue so all children get a chance.

Display
Create a display of different types of fastenings which the children can use. Place an enlarged 'How to do it poster – RS2' on the wall or cut each picture up and then attach clothing with zips and buttons, a range of belts with buckles and shoe lacing cards onto the wall or on table below for the children to use.

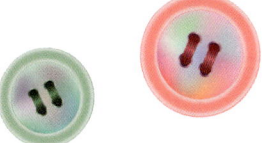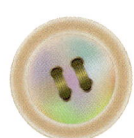

All Done Up

Clara, do your coat up.
ZIP, ZIP, ZIP
But how do I do it?
ZIP, ZIP, ZIP

Put the zip together,
Pull it to the top.
Now you should be ready,
To go out to the shops.

Johnny, put your shirt on.
BUTTON, BUTTON, BUTTON
But how do I do it?
BUTTON, BUTTON, BUTTON

Open up the button holes,
Push the buttons through.
Now you should be ready,
To go out to the zoo.

Becky, do your belt up.
BUCKLE, BUCKLE, BUCKLE
But how do I do it?
BUCKLE, BUCKLE, BUCKLE

Put it through the buckle,
Make it nice and tight.
Now you should be ready,
To go and fly your kite.

Charlie, do your laces up.
LACES, LACES, LACES
But how do I do it?
LACES, LACES, LACES.

Cross them over, make a loop,
Go round it and then pull.
Now you should be ready,
To go and play football.

Using storytelling to talk about...**Health & Self care**

Related activities within the learning environment

Literacy

Let the children make little instruction books on how to do up one of the fastenings. Write a simple caption underneath each picture, which they can either copy or trace over.

Mathematics

Give the children a tray of buttons to sort and classify. Let them count the buttons. How many can they count?

Let the children investigate the length of different belts and laces. Invite them to put them in size order. Ask the children to guess and then investigate how many laces tied together can match their own height.

Art & Craft

Help the children trace round their shoes on cardboard and then cut out the shapes. Use a hole punch to make holes in the cardboard shoe and thread them with laces. Let the children keep the lace cards to practise doing up shoelaces.

Provide the children with lengths of zips and a range of buttons to make fun interactive collages.

Games

Use the cards from 'Which is the right one? – RS3' for a range of games, e.g. create two sets to play 'pairs', match the fastener to the correct item, snap etc. The children could draw in the missing fasteners on the clothing and bag pictures. They could also use the fastener pictures to help them find items in the room that have the same fasteners.

Exploring

Set out a table with zips, lace cards, different types of buckles and clothing with buttons. Encourage the children to explore and take their time to work out how to use the different fasteners correctly.

Role-play corner

Put out dressing up clothes and accessories that need to be zipped, buttoned or fastened in other ways. Encourage the children to help each other get dressed.

Small world

Set out play figures with a mix of clothes. Encourage the children to dress the dolls using the buttons, Velcro and so on.

Resource sheet 1

'All Done Up' pictures

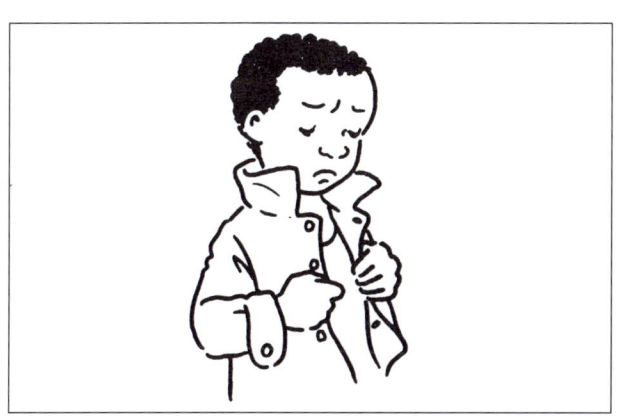

Resource sheet 2

'How to do it' poster

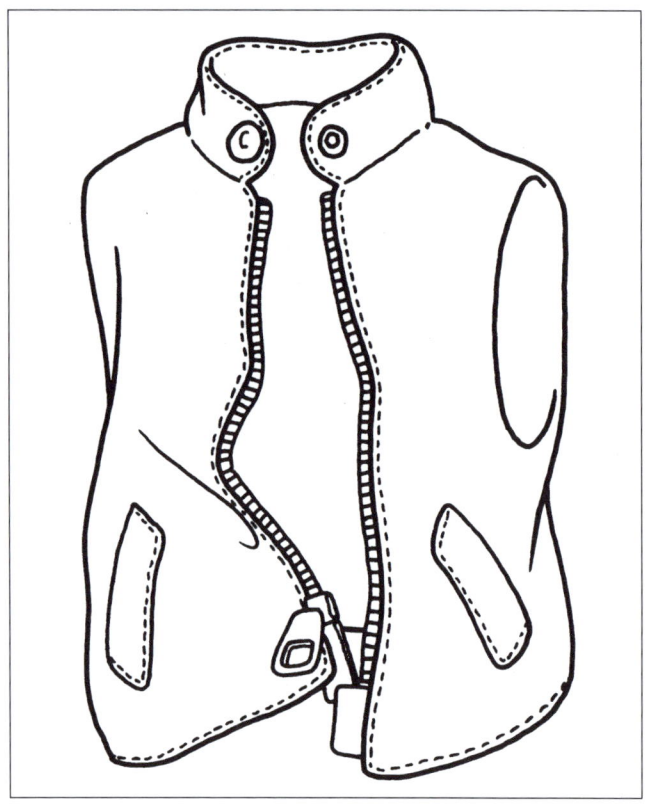

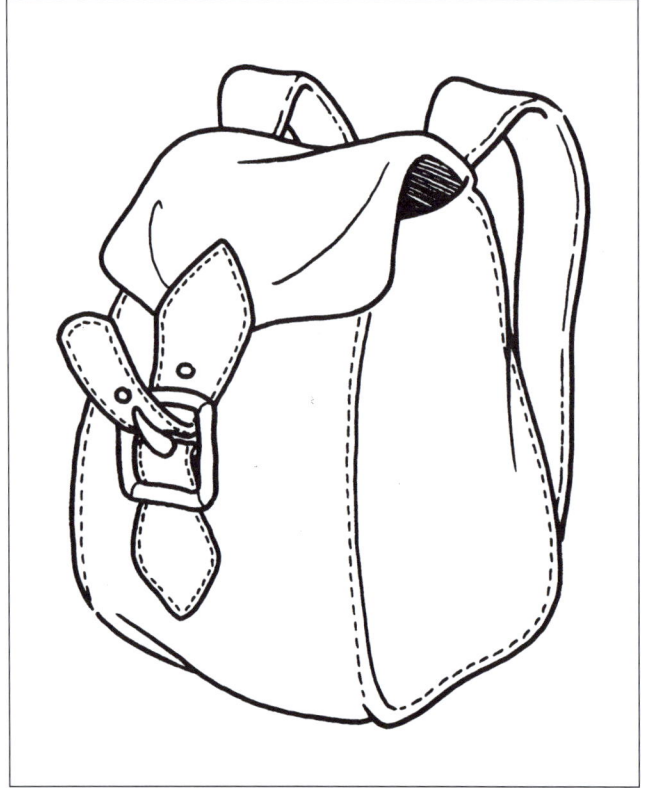
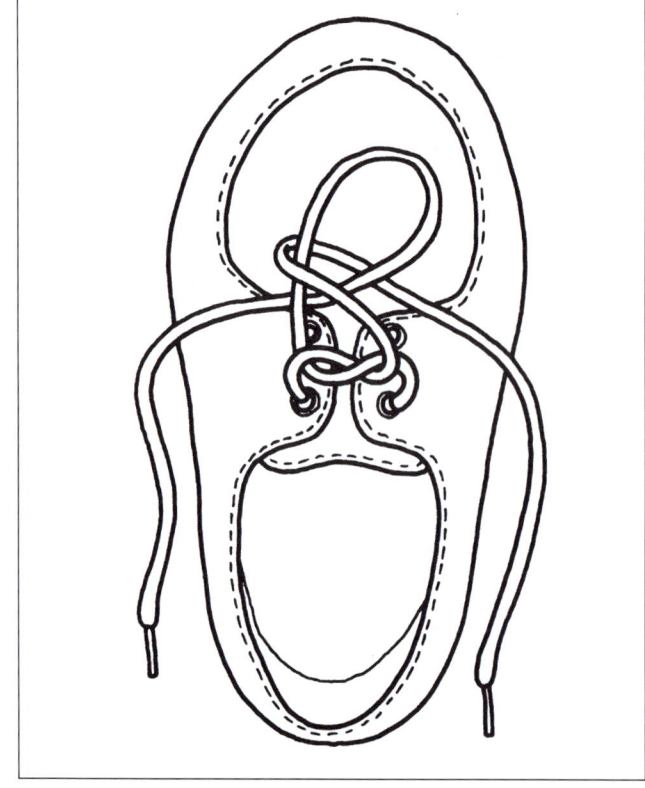

Resource sheet 3

Which is the right one?

Draw lines to match the pictures.

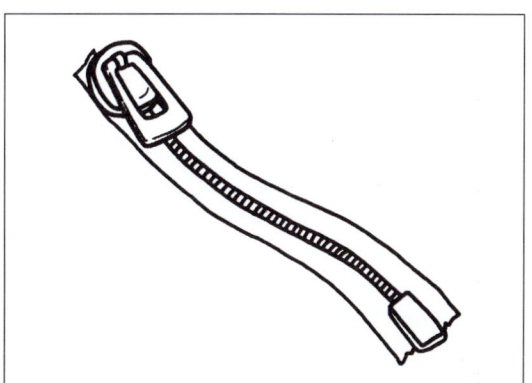

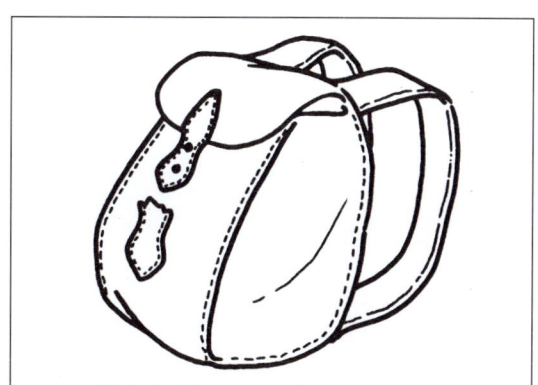

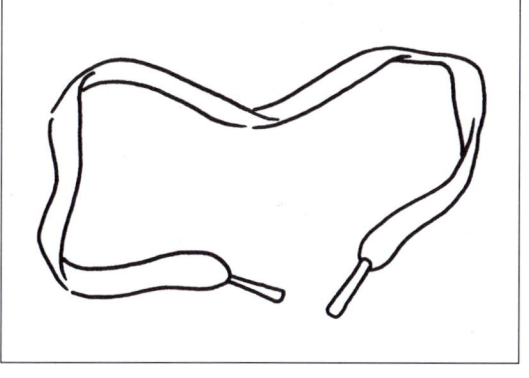

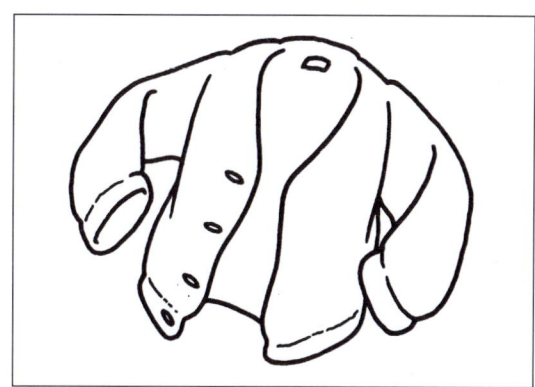

EYFS Learning Areas Reference Chart

	Star Jumpers Club	At the Market	Zig Gets Lost	What Shall I Do?	Snozzle the Sneezing Giant	Our Teeth	Changing Weather	All Done Up
Health and self-care	Story	Song	Story	Song	Story	Poem	Story	Poem
MANAGING SELF								
Be confident to try new activities	X			X		X	X	X
Show independence, resilience and perseverance in the face of challenge	X		X				X	X
Know right from wrong and try to behave accordingly				X				
Manage their own basic hygiene and personal needs, including dressing, going to the toilet				X	X	X	X	X
Understanding the importance of healthy food choices		X				X		
PERSONAL, SOCIAL AND EMOTIONAL DEVELOPMENT AREAS								
Self-Regulation	X	X	X	X	X	X	X	X
Building Relationships	X	X	X	X	X		X	X
OTHER LEARNING AREAS								
Communication and Language	X	X	X	X	X	X	X	X
Physical Development	X			X		X	X	X
Literacy	X	X	X	X	X	X	X	X
Numeracy	X	X	X	X	X	X	X	X
Understanding the World	X	X	X			X	X	
Expressive Arts and Design	X	X	X	X	X	X	X	X

Storytelling assessment record

Personal, social and emotional development		
EYFS learning and development area: Theme: Story, poem or song: Title: Date:		
	OBSERVATIONS	**IDEAS FOR NEXT SESSION**
Preparation: learnt story/poem thoroughly; choice of props, resources, placement of resources before story time.		
Introduction: good use of anecdote or prop to introduce theme or story/poem/song; engagement and interaction of children; link into telling or performing main story/poem.		
Group/child engagement: eye contact; awareness of children with learning difficulties; held children's attention (all or parts); ability to cope with interruptions or unsettled behaviour. Flexibility in performance.		
Group interaction: join in with repetitive text, sounds; follow action movements; share and use props.		
Voice: clear and strong, use of voice tone and volume; use of voice to signal interactions or repetitive texts.		
Body language: clear use of body actions to enhance performance.		
Pace and rhythm: clear start and ending of story; consistent pace of storytelling; clear difference in verse and chorus.		
Characters: use of different voices for different characters; use of voice to show moods and reactions; use of voice to emphasise rhythm.		
Ending of the session: clear ending of session; good feedback and discussion from children about the story or poem/song.		

Using storytelling to talk about…**Health & Self care**

Observation suggestions

Title and theme	Observation suggestion
Star Jumpers Club – story Theme: Being active	• Note what physical activities the children do or like to do. Are they any new ones they would like to try? • Note how the children join in with the story and their ability to join in with the movements.
At the Food Market – song Theme: Different foods	• Note which children understand the importance of eating healthy food. • Listen to children's experiences of eating foods from different cultures.
Zig Gets Lost – story Theme: Keeping safe	• Make a note on which children were able to understand and talk about ways to stay safe. • Observe if the children ask for help during role play time.
What Shall I do? – song Theme: Getting clean	• Observe which children know how to clean their hands and faces. • Note which children feel confident in following simple 2-3 verbal instructions.
Snoozle the Sneezing Giant – story Theme: Using a hankie	• Note whether children understand how germs spread and why we use a hankie. • Look for examples of the children's understanding of the story message and the good and bad actions of the characters.
Our Teeth – poem Theme: Caring for our teeth	• Look for children's understanding of why we need to clean our teeth. • Listen to the children sharing their tooth brushing routines. Do some children need extra help?
Changing Weather – story Theme: Dressing for the weather	• Observe whether the children understand the need to change their clothing for different weather conditions. Can they make their own decisions to make the changes? • Listen and note the children's abilities to recall and retell the story using role play and discussion.
All Done Up – poem Theme: Different clothes fastenings	• Note which clothes fastenings the children are confident in using and the ones that they need practice with. • Note if they ask for help when they need to do up a difficult fastening.

Observation record

Name/s *(child, pair or group)* :

Age/s:

Story or poem/song title:

Main learning outcomes:

Child/children's understanding and comments about the main theme in the story or poem/song.

Further activities observations, e.g. how are the children showing what they've learnt in other activities?

Further support or needs: